GOD'S COMING

AN ADVENT STUDY
—— FOR ADULTS ——

Reginald Mallett

🎼 Abingdon Press

GOD'S COMING IN CHRIST:
AN ADVENT STUDY FOR ADULTS

Copyright © 1995 by Abingdon Press

Library of Congress Cataloging-in-Publication Data

Mallett, Reginald.
  God's coming in Christ : an Advent study for adults / Reginald
Mallett.
    p.   cm.
ISBN 0-687-00574-4

  1. Advent—Meditations.   2. Advent—Study and teaching.
I. Title
BV40.M35 1995
242' .33—dc20   95-11871
                                                                        CIP

95 96 97 98 99 00 01 02 03 04—10 9 8 7 6 5 4 3 2 1

MANUFACTURED IN THE UNITED STATES OF AMERICA

With love and gratitude to my wife, Brenda,
who has been, as always, a source of encouragement
and support

CONTENTS

INTRODUCTION

Advent: A Time of Waiting

"It takes the waiting out of wanting." So trumpeted the advertising slogan used to launch a new charge card. Its appeal is obvious. When we want something, we want it *right now!* We can't wait. Let's live now and pay later!

"I'm so excited, Doctor, I don't know that I will be able to wait another seven months!" The young mother-to-be was flushed with delight when I gave her the result of the pregnancy test. I searched for a suitable response and finally said something like this: "I think you will find that the waiting will give you and your husband time to prepare for the baby's coming. Make the most of these days of waiting. Don't wish them away. They are an important part of the experience."

Of course I could understand her excited impatience. Anyone could. It was entirely human. Yet the truth is that the waiting was essential. Changes would take place in her body and in her emotions. She and her husband would need to prepare themselves for new responsibilities, and all kinds of other preparations would need to be made. The joy that would eventually be theirs would be made all the more complete if they used the time of waiting to the full.

Much of the joy in an event is subtly bound up in the waiting. This is as true of having a baby as it is of buying a new car or of being reunited with a loved one who has been away. *Waiting heightens the joy.*

Advent is a time of waiting, a time for reflection: What is this all about? It is a window through which we can gaze in devotion and wonder upon the plan of God and marvel at the promise that just as God came in humility in the Christ child, so also God will come again in power.

It would be unrealistic and naïve to ignore the commercial pressures of this season. The power of advertising through the media is immense. We are bombarded with information about so many things without which our Christmas, so we are told, will be incomplete. These subtle persuaders make it difficult, if not impossible, to be faithful to the discipline of "Advent waiting." We cannot insulate ourselves from the predominant culture, which seems determined to turn the whole of the month of December into a pre-Christmas shopping spree.

But it would be wrong to capitulate and give in to these external forces. As Christians we cannot feebly submit without a fight and allow this holy season to become completely secularized. Advent is not just a number of shopping days to Christmas. It is a time to prepare for the coming of the King. For the sake of our spiritual health we must try to adjust the balance—*to put back the waiting into wanting.*

In a stressful and hurried world it is difficult to find time for reflection. We rush into worship and then wonder why sometimes we get little from it. We deny ourselves moments for quiet reflection and meditation in which we can discover new perspectives and truths about ourselves and about God, and then we wonder why our prayers seem mechanical and dry.

Without a doubt, the days of December are frenzied. Most of us are caught up in the dizzying spiral of pre-Christmas activity. Each year it seems to get worse. We resolve that next year we will make an earlier start on the preparations. We are catapulted into a frenzy of writing cards, buying presents, arranging parties, putting up decorations, rehearsing at church for the Christmas music or pageant, making costumes for the children's Nativity play—the list is seemingly endless. Suddenly it is Christmas Eve. Now we are dashing to church, exhausted. There hasn't been time to listen to the message of the angels. We have not been able to reflect on the wonder and mystery of this marvelous event we are celebrating.

Some people almost dread Christmas. "To be perfectly honest," one person said to me, "I feel a sense of relief by the time I take the Christmas decorations down."

What a pity! The real meaning of the season has been missed. The church clings to Advent because we need it. Advent is a wonderful gift: four weeks in which to think about God's coming in Christ; four weeks in which to recall how God's people were prepared through the ages for the greatest event in history; four weeks in which to look inward and upward; four weeks in which to consider that we live in God's world and the future rests secure in God's hands; four weeks in which to remember that just as the road of the past led to Bethlehem, so the road of the present and future leads to the fulfillment of the plan of God. Knowing that Christ will come again in glory gives us hope in the midst of the darkness of cynicism and despair. *We need this time of waiting.*

In what follows, we will explore some of the great Advent themes. We will see how an observance of this season makes Christmas and its festivities all the more meaningful. We will seek to recapture the sense of longing for deliverance which the people of God experienced. We will see that the fulfillment of this longing brings joy and celebration. In each of the four lessons, which correspond to the four weeks of Advent, material is provided for discussion in a group setting. Questions facilitate group discussion and devotional aids can be used during the week following each lesson. This study is intended to add to the joy of the Nativity. By traveling prayerfully through the weeks of Advent, we will find that we are ready to welcome our Savior when Christmas comes.

THE FIRST WEEK OF ADVENT

God's Answer to the Aching Heart

My soul waits for the Lord / more than watchmen
wait for the morning. (Ps. 130:6 NIV)

I had been in my job as a junior hospital doctor for only a week when I admitted Doris. She was no stranger to hospitals or to pain. The notes of her previous treatments filled two thick volumes. What impressed me was her courage and cheerfulness as we talked about her problems. She shrugged off my sympathy. "Being here is not so bad," she said.

"But there must be something you really don't like about hospitals, isn't there?" I asked. For a moment she became serious. "Well, since you asked me, I will tell you. There is one thing that terrifies me." I expected her to talk about the necessary unpleasant procedures in her treatment. I was wrong. In a whisper she said, "I dread the nights."

She explained that during the day her pain was bearable. There were many distractions such as visitors coming and going, doctors and nurses flitting in and out of her room, volunteers coming around with hospital books. At night it was different. Then the hospital was silent, apart from regular checks by the night nurse. Then the pain seemed so much worse. "I find the nights in the hospital are so long," she said. "I just ache for the morning."

The psalmist is writing of his deep yearning for God. He looks around for a human analogy and thinks about watchmen guarding a city. For them the greatest danger comes at night. Enemies often use the darkness as a cloak under which to take the watchmen by surprise. Anxiously they keep their vigil, longing for the morning. For them, as for Doris, the night watch seems endless. They crave the gray light of dawn and the promise of daylight. "My longing for God," the psalmist says, "is that kind of deep pining. I wait for God more eagerly than watchmen wait for the morning."

Studies have shown that a surprisingly large number of people, some of them quite worldly, have experienced moments when they are aware of a spiritual dimension. Sometimes these moments have taken them by surprise, and they are embarrassed to talk about them. Often they are just brief flashes of insight, fleeting and rare, but they bring with them a spiritual longing.

Such moments are unpredictable. They are *transcendent,* outside what would be considered normal experience. Their power and influence defy explanation and definition. They cannot be produced to order.

9

They just happen, and when they come they awaken a hunger for God.

The psalmist caught a glimpse of God, and his whole being cried out, "This was real! This made sense of life! I want more! *My soul waits for the Lord more than watchmen wait for the morning!*"

Have you known such a moment? Perhaps it was when you were waiting for the doctor to bring you news of a test; or one evening when you put your new baby to bed and, sitting quietly, you were suddenly awestruck by the wonder of life and the solemnity of your responsibility. Perhaps it occurred during worship in church. When it happened, it was overwhelming. It may have disappeared as suddenly as it came, but the memory of it lingers. It was indescribable. It was *transcendent.* In that moment, perhaps much to your own amazement, you found yourself beginning to long for God.

We must cling to these deep longings and bring them to our Advent observance. They lie at the heart of the season. In monasteries and other Christian communities across the centuries, the seven "O"s or antiphons were sung during these days to express the longing for Christ to come and complete his work. The New Testament ends, just before its final benediction, with this note of longing: *"Even so, come, Lord Jesus"* (Rev. 22:20*b* KJV).

The coming of Jesus is God's answer to the aching heart of the believer.

David Brainerd was born in 1718 and died before he was thirty. In that short life, lived entirely in his native America, he left a record of Christian service which remains a model for all who long to share the gospel of Christ.

Racked by tuberculosis, never free from pain, often exposed to terrible dangers and privations, Brainerd traveled among the Native American tribes. He was driven by one consuming desire: to bring light to his Native American brothers and sisters. The entry in his journal for February 15, 1745, reads:

> This evening I was much assisted in meditating on that precious text: Jesus stood and cried, If any man thirst, let him come unto Me and drink. I longed to proclaim such grace to the whole world of sinners. (F. W. Boreham, *Casket of Cameos* [London: Epworth Press, 1926], p. 29)

Across the centuries the saints have longed for goodness to triumph over evil, for love to overcome hate, for gentleness to replace viciousness and force, for truth to remove falsehood. They have made no headlines, but their longings expressed in their lives have been enriching and ennobling influences. Theirs is an inner aching. It is like the longing with which the watchman waited for the morning. To such as them the joyful message of Advent rings out. In Jesus the realization of their dreams has dawned.

The glad message of Advent is that God began to meet the longing of the believer in the coming of his Son in Bethlehem, and in his final coming, this humble beginning will be gloriously completed. Advent cautions us: Do not despise the day of small beginnings. In a child born so humbly, light has come at last. The world may not heed the announcement of the angel. Other events that are considered more momentous may preoccupy the minds of men and women. But what began in Bethlehem makes all other events trivial by comparison.

The coming of Jesus is God's answer to the aching heart of the worshiper.

The Old Testament writers frequently expressed their dismay at the unreality of worship. It had become mechanical, degenerating into the performance of religious exercises.

The prophet Malachi had the heart of a true worshiper, and he was disturbed by what he saw in the temple. Although people came to worship, their hearts were not in it. Their real worship lay elsewhere, in their businesses, their farms, and their pursuit of worldly pleasure. By attending the ceremonies in the temple, they created a false appearance of spirituality. Nor were the priests any better. They treated the handling of holy things just like any secular job! Malachi was appalled by the sight of both priests and people coming into the presence of God, who read the secrets of all their hearts, and making a pretense of worship.

He knew that behind their pious words lay evil habits and thoughts. They said they longed for God and were seeking him in his temple, but really that was the last thing they wanted. With the deep, passionate longing of a true worshiper, Malachi cried, "The Lord whom you seek will suddenly come to his temple. The messenger of the covenant in whom you delight—indeed, he is coming, says the LORD of hosts. But who can endure the day of his coming, and who can stand when he appears? For he is like a refiner's fire" (Mal. 3:1-2). Yes, God is coming, the prophet says, but you won't like it when he arrives!

If we are honest, we will admit that much of our worship is hollow. We just go through the motions. We attend church regularly. We read our Bible. We may even say a prayer. But our hearts are not in it. We are not deliberately insincere. It is simply that we live in a frantic, busy world, and our lives have become crowded. We are preoccupied with things, which in themselves are perfectly wholesome and good—our work, our families, our social obligations. There doesn't seem to be room for anything else.

Then it happens! Suddenly, when we least expect it, we have one of those transcendent moments. We feel an inner restlessness. "Surely there is more to life than this!" we cry. In that instant we reach out for God. We sense a hunger for immortality and feel that we are made not just for today but for eternity. And in that moment we find ourselves longing for God.

To catch the spirit of Advent is to share the longing of the psalmist at worship, who aches for God: "My soul waits for the Lord more than watchmen wait for the morning." And ringing across the ages comes the glad assurance: "In Christ, he has come. He comes. He will come." And he is seen by the humble in spirit and the pure in heart.

On my desk is a photograph of the impressive work *The Christus* by Bertal Thorwaldsen. My friend A. S. Wood in his book *For All Seasons* (London: Hodder and Stoughton, 1979, p. 169) notes how the head of this striking figure of Christ inclines, so that it is difficult to see Christ's expression without stooping and looking up. Wood said that a man was standing before this statue one day when a helpful attendant plucked his sleeve and said, "Excuse me, Sir. You cannot see his face without kneeling at his feet."

Christ is coming. He is the answer to the aching heart of the worshiper. And this Advent, those who are ready to kneel at his feet will see him.

The coming of Jesus is God's answer to the aching heart of the sinner.

There are some whose hearts ache for something much closer to home. They are carrying a secret burden of guilt; they long for some memory of the past to be blotted out.

A close minister friend, D. A. Greeves, told me of something that happened when he was a boy. Although it was a trivial matter, it made a permanent impression on him.

His father was a minister. His mother had a friend who helped her in the home. This friend was a skillful seamstress, and each summer she made beach clothes for the children to wear on vacation at a coastal resort. One summer she was making my friend his first pair of shorts with pockets. To a child, pockets are a part of life's magic! They provide a home for all kinds of treasures.

My friend watched her with excitement as the shorts took shape. It was then that he said the sort of thing that is likely to come from any tactless, uninhibited child. Staring at her, he said, "Why is your nose like a strawberry?" He had not meant to be unkind or rude, but he could tell from his mother's cry of horror that he had said something terrible and he fled from the room. His mother came after him and sent him back to offer an apology, which was graciously accepted.

The matter was forgotten until vacation time.

The night they arrived at the vacation cottage, the suitcases were unpacked. The first thing my friend did was to put on his new shorts. He put his hands in the pockets and felt something round and hard in one of them. It was a coin! A message from the gracious seamstress. She was saying, "I love you, and I forgive you. As a token of my forgiveness I want you to have this gift." She knew he wanted to be forgiven, and she had done something about it.

My friend said to me, "When I take Holy Communion, I think of her. It is as though God were saying, 'I love you and I forgive you—and as a token of my forgiveness, I am giving you myself.'"

Have you had moments when you longed to feel God embracing you and saying, "I love you, and I forgive you"? Have you found sometimes that longing is so intense that you could say you long for God *more than watchmen for the morning?*

Then here is marvelous news: Advent proclaims that God has come to you! God came in Jesus and continues to come whenever we pause and open up our lives. God will come again in glory to complete his glorious work. And as he comes he brings healing and forgiveness. God is the answer to the aching heart.

STUDY QUESTIONS

1. Read Isaiah 51:4-8. Here assurance is given that God's kingdom is coming, will last forever, and is intended for *all*. In your Advent preparations, how do you think of the hungry, the homeless, the dispossessed, or the unbeliever? Does your heart ache for them also to share in this glorious hope? What actions can you take in response?

2. Read Isaiah 52:7-10. The waiting of the watchmen is rewarded as a herald comes over the mountains to announce God's coming. It has been said that "expectation is the parent of experience." What are you expecting this Advent? What steps can you take to live expectantly each day, trusting God in all things?

3. Read Romans 13:8-14. (It is helpful to read this passage along with Matthew 25:31-40.) Paul reminds us that the new age of the Kingdom has already dawned. As we await the return of Christ in glory, are we living as "Kingdom people"? What is your evidence? Think of at least three things you can do this week which will identify you as a "Kingdom person"—such as bridging a broken relationship, visiting a friendless sick person, or encouraging a downcast person with a call or a letter.

4. Read Mark 13:32-37. Since we do not know when God will finally bring the present age to a close, we ought to live each day as if it were the day of Christ's return. Consider your agenda for today. What alterations would you make if you knew Christ were coming today? Would you make time to be alone with God? Would you want to remove some undesirable thing from your home or your life? Would you be more concerned to share your faith with others?

FOCUS FOR THE WEEK: BEING "KINGDOM PEOPLE"

Is your longing for the coming of Christ expressed in what you are and what you do? Would you be ashamed or delighted if Christ came today? Would you welcome a scrutiny of your personal discipleship? What about your home life? What about your concern for the marginalized? What about your involvement in the struggle for justice and world peace? If your heart aches for his coming, then how does this affect your life? Is Advent longing being translated into Advent living?

THE SECOND WEEK OF ADVENT

The Voice in the Desert

*Jesus began to speak to the crowds about John:
"What did you go out into the wilderness to look at. . . . a prophet?
Yes, I tell you, and more than a prophet."* (Matt. 11:7-9)

When God prepares, God prepares thoroughly.

I first met Janet when she was a student nurse. She already had two nursing qualifications. She was a registered nurse and a state certified midwife. She was still unsure, however, what she ought to do with her life. After some time in reflection and prayer, she felt a call to return to training and acquire a third qualification as a certified pediatric nurse.

One evening after I had preached a sermon on the call of Moses, she came and talked to me about her future. She felt that God was prodding her, but she was not sure what her next step in obedience ought to be. As we talked I felt a strong urge to suggest that she talk to the medical secretary of her church's overseas division. As a result, several months later she was on her way to a mission hospital in Africa. There she was put in charge of the general nursing.

She had been there only a short while when a new maternity wing was opened. Someone was needed who had the qualifications to supervise not only the general nursing but also the new midwifery department. Janet was exactly the right person.

A year later a children's block was added. Now someone was needed who had the unusual qualifications of general nursing, midwifery, and pediatrics. Janet was there, ready to step into the position. Precisely the right person was in the right place at the right time. God had prepared the way.

During Advent, Christians honor John the Baptist. They remember how God used him to prepare the way for the coming of Jesus. How John did this has been an inspiration to the community of faith ever since.

John prepared the way by living a godly life.

In an age of corruption, John the Baptist appeared as a clean, bracing breath of mountain air. In his passionate embrace of goodness, he spoke out fearlessly against every form of corruption without considering his own safety. On one occasion the religious leaders from Jerusalem came to hear him. A lesser man would have been flattered and would have expressed appreciation at the honor their presence signified. John, however, was uncompromising and forthright: "You brood of vipers! Who warned you to flee from the wrath to come?" (Matt. 3:7).

A great preacher, referring on one occasion to the vehemence with which John denounced sin, said, "The heart that does not know this kind of anger is the heart which is not pure." John's devotion was complete, and the impact of his godliness prepared the way for Jesus.

I once heard E. Stanley Jones, world-renowned author-evangelist, tell of visiting a Chinese village. He spoke at an open-air meeting with the assistance of an interpreter. In simple words he told the story of Jesus. He described the Savior's ministry, his humble way of life, his going about doing good, his love for the ordinary people—healing the sick, welcoming the outcast, and lifting the fallen. When he had finished, a man came to him in great excitement. Through the interpreter the man said in an eager voice, "What you say is true. I have met him. The one of whom you speak lives in the village over the mountains."

Jones was intrigued. He thought at first that the poor man was suffering from delusions. It turned out, however, that he was a respected farmer who, in selling his produce, traveled much farther than his neighbors. He told Jones his story, the gist of which was:

> When I was journeying over the mountains near the village where the man of whom you speak lives, I fell and broke my arm. I tried to travel on but was overcome by pain and collapsed. This man found me, took me to his cabin, fed me, and fixed my arm. Yes, I know him, although his name is different from the one which you used.

So Jones made a point of traveling over the mountains to look for the village the farmer described. When he found it, he discovered the people to be in deep mourning. They listened intently to his message and then explained that they had heard some of it before. They told him that they had heard it from "the man with the stick" whose recent death they were now lamenting. He learned that this man with the stick was the local doctor who had become a Christian years before and had spent his life in service to the village. In his later years he had walked with the aid of a stick. Jones concluded, "The radiance of that good man's life made the people receptive to the message which I now brought to them." The man with the stick had prepared the way for the evangelist by the quality of his life.

The philosopher David Hume used to spend vacations in Haddington, a little town close to Edinburgh in Scotland. On those occasions it was his custom to attend the parish church. Once someone in his party referred to it when they met socially after the service. Laughingly the man said, "Of course you don't believe all the stuff which that old man was saying, do you?" David Hume replied, "Perhaps not." "Then why go?" asked his skeptical companion. "I go because that good man believes it and lives it," he replied, adding in an undertone, "and I wish to God I did."

When I was a university student, a visiting speaker told of a newspaper reporter who was conducting an in-depth study of a Roman Catholic order of nuns. These Sisters were working in a very deprived inner-city area. The reporter could not believe any group of people could be so utterly unselfish. He was convinced that the loving philanthropy and apparent tenderness of these women was just a cover for obtaining financial support for their institution.

The Sisters agreed to his request to accompany one of the nuns in her work on a typical day. She took him down some of the most dilapidated streets he had ever seen. In the basement of one house was a man who was terminally ill. The reporter was accustomed to grim conditions, but these made even him wince. The dirt and odor were overpowering. Vermin scurried away as they approached. The sick man, lying on a bundle of rags, was indescribably dirty. He was trembling. His condition was the product of poverty, disease, alcohol, and drugs.

The reporter watched as the nun rolled up her sleeves, picked up a bowl, filled it with water from a tap upstairs, and began to wash the sick man. Suddenly the man jerked up. "Sister," he whimpered, "I am frightened." The cynical reporter later wrote, "I stared in unbelief as I saw this refined, cultured woman take that filthy wreck of a man and hold him in her arms like a baby. Suddenly that hovel became heaven because love was there." He was overwhelmed by the goodness he saw.

John the Baptist had that kind of impact. By his quality of life he prepared the way for Jesus. During Advent, Christians are called to share in that ministry. We are called to prepare the way by the kind of lives we live. What a challenge!

John prepared the way by challenging people's sins.

John the Baptist had the courage to challenge sin wherever he found it. The king's palace was no exception.

King Herod had seduced his brother's wife and taken her to live with him. Although the people were outraged, their religious leaders were silent. They were afraid of the king. They knew that he could be violent and ruthless if provoked. But this wild preacher from the wilderness did not consider his own safety. He had eyes only for God.

With outspoken courage, John denounced the king and his "wife," Herodias. For this defiance he paid dearly. Neither Herod nor Herodias ever forgot it. Eventually his fearlessness cost him first his liberty and then his life. John was a man of the hills and the open spaces. For him the confines of a prison cell must have been worse than the death which came so cruelly as a result of the scheming woman he had so courageously denounced. Yet he sacrificed the free life in the open air for loyalty to the truth. He had eyes for none but God. He sought not popular approval, only the smile of heaven.

In *For All Seasons,* A. S. Wood tells the story of one of Verdi's operas. The composer was young, and this particular work was said to have been produced in a hurry. Verdi knew that it was not his best. It was staged for the first time in Florence. As the final curtain came down, the audience gave it an undeserved ovation. But, it is said, Verdi was oblivious to the popular verdict. He had eyes for only one man; he looked to where he sat. All the plaudits of the crowd would not compensate for the lack of this one man's approval. The man was Rossini, the great composer, and Rossini was not smiling!

In Advent we salute the forerunner who prepared the way by challenging the people's sins. He was not after the popular vote. He desired only to serve God. As we observe Advent, John challenges our shabby compromises and our tolerance of the second-rate. By what he was, he is a standing rebuke to the dubious standards of our day.

By holding John the Baptist before us, Advent shakes us out of our complacency. It causes us to review our slide into the tolerance of evil. It calls us back to a mission of purity. Do we have the moral courage to accept the challenge?

John the Baptist prepared the way by pointing to Christ.

A number of years ago a couple I know went to adopt a baby after being on the waiting list of the adoption agency for a long time. A kind official led them up a flight of stairs to a waiting room at the agency. After a few minutes they heard someone entering the next room. It was the young student mother who was bringing her baby for adoption. Our friends heard a muffled conversation and, a few minutes later, her convulsive sobbing as she left the office.

The official then took them next door. In a crib was a six-week-old baby boy. On a chair beside it was a brown paper bag containing a change of clothes and two letters. In one of these, addressed to the new parents, the baby's mother expressed her gratitude for their providing a home for her baby and so giving her a chance to start her life afresh. She went on to acknowledge that under the terms of the adoption, common at that time, each would never know who the other was. Then the young mother added one request: Would they allow her son to read the other letter on his eighteenth birthday? She assured them that she had not included any information about her identity.

The request was honored. By now that young man will have read the message his mother wrote on the day when, with a breaking heart, she parted with him.

I wonder what she wrote. If I had to condense all that I feel about life and love into a few precious words, what would I say? I would have no time for trivialities. I would not be concerned about economics, politics, the weather, the size of my house, or the kind of car I drive. I would concentrate on profundities, on what I believe life to be all about and what things I consider the "essentials."

John in the desert was in the great tradition of the Hebrew prophets. He was aware that time was running out. He had no time for peripheral matters. Soon the sword of Herod's guard would flash, and he would lie silent in the grave.

Superficial people came out from Jerusalem to see him. They were intrigued by the strange phenomenon of a wild man preaching repentance. They were fascinated by frivolous things such as his dress, his diet, and his fierce declamatory oratory. They wanted to interview him and then tell all their friends about their remarkable experience. "Who are you?" they asked. His answer was curt: "I am not the Christ." "Are you Elijah?" "No!" "Then who are you?" they persisted. John answered, "I am a voice" (see John 1:19-23).

There comes a moment when the preacher longs for his or her hearers to lose sight of everything except the message. "Don't listen to my accent. Don't look at my clothes. Don't comment on my style. Don't compare me with other preachers. Don't search my biographical details for my university pedigree. Just listen to what I am saying. *I am a voice.*"

And it was John's crowning glory that he saw something that no other had recognized. Others had foretold that God would intervene in human affairs. They had predicted that the Messiah would come. In the popular mind the Messiah would come at the head of a conquering army—the Lion of Judah to the fight! But this wild man from the wilderness saw into the heart of his nation and into the mind of his God. This insight he has left for us and our children forever. "Here is the Lamb of God who takes away the sin of the world!" (John 1:29).

In Advent, as we salute the forerunner, John the Baptist, we are reminded that there is no greater privilege given to anyone this side of heaven than to point to the Lamb of God, who takes away the sin of the world. Everything else the church of God may do—build hospitals, open orphanages, establish hospices for the dying, feed the starving, comfort the homeless—must flow from this one central mission, to point to the Lamb of God who takes away the sin of the world. This Advent, we can prepare the way of the Lord by pointing to the Christ.

STUDY QUESTIONS

1. Have you ever had an experience like the one Janet had of being in the right place at the right time? How can you be spiritually sensitive to such opportunities in your life?

2. Read Isaiah 40:1-11. The prophet says the way needs to be prepared and obstacles removed so that the exiles can return home. How is God similarly calling the church to assist in the return of spiritual exiles who have wandered into unbelief? What are some of the hindrances to faith that these exiles may encounter? What can you identify in your personal or corporate life as a Christian which might make it difficult for another to return to faith?

3. Read John 1:19-28. By his life as well as by his words, John the Baptist prepared men and women for the message of Jesus. When people get to know you, do they recognize that you are a Christian? What are the things in your life which draw attention to Jesus? In what ways do you prepare others for the message of Jesus?

4. Read Matthew 14:1-12. John preached repentance and was fearless in denouncing what was wrong. What do you believe are the great moral issues on which Christians should take a stand? What can we do to help make the influences of the media more wholesome? What social injustices cause you to feel a righteous anger? Is there anything you can do about them?

5. Read Romans 12:9-21. John's preaching and his living complemented each other. Can you think of any area where your words and deeds contradict each other? What resolutions can you make so that this Advent your life can be used by God to prepare the way for others to see the Christ?

FOCUS FOR THE WEEK: SHARING JOHN'S MINISTRY

This Advent be aware that every day you will meet people who have turned away from Christ. Although some have been lured by wrongful desires, many have been battered and bruised by tough experiences such as sickness, bereavement, or the unfaithfulness of someone dear to them. Others may have been disappointed by the quality of the lives of some professing Christians they know. As you start each day, remind yourself of the way in which John prepared the way for Jesus. By the testimony of your life in faithful Advent living, you can share in John's ministry.

THE THIRD WEEK OF ADVENT

Rejoicing in the Savior's Coming

The LORD is king! Let the earth rejoice; . . . / righteousness and justice are the foundation of his throne. (Ps. 97:1-2)

A delightful musical from the early sixties was recently revived in England. It is called *Pickwick* and is based on the novel by Charles Dickens. The song from the show that our family enjoys most is entitled "If I Ruled the World." In it a smiling Mr. Pickwick announces that there would be more happiness in the world if he were in charge.

The words of the song strike a chord with most of us at this time of the year because happiness is at the top of our agenda. Our friends greet us with the words "Merry Christmas." One of the most popular songs of the season expresses the wish, "May your days be merry and bright, and may all your Christmases be white."

The church joins in with this note of gladness. The theme for the Third Sunday in Advent is rejoicing. This day used to be known as "Gaudete Sunday" from the opening word "Rejoice" in the Latin introit. It is the church's recognition that the Christmas celebration is near.

Once we reach the month of December, the countdown to Bethlehem has begun. Little fingers are opening the windows of Advent calendars and working out the number of days to Christmas. This is the season to be jolly. We cannot stand the thought of people being unhappy in the midst of our festivities.

I once served a mission church in a deprived part of London. I quickly discovered why, like many other charities, it was the Mission's policy to appeal to the general public for financial assistance in the weeks close to Christmas. Seasonal goodwill brought with it greater generosity.

We all receive many appeals during Advent from deserving causes. We read heartrending stories of needy people, especially children. The plight of abused, blind, or sick children seems particularly poignant at this time of the year when we want them to be happy.

There have been moments when, surrounded by these Advent appeals which describe so much pain and need in the world, I have been tempted to share Mr. Pickwick's belief that the world would be a happier place if I were its ruler. I would ensure that children not be born blind or suffer from cancer. At a stroke I would provide homes for the homeless. I would make hospitals redundant because I would banish illness. There would be no mourning parents placing flowers on tiny graves this Christmas; instead, they would be filling the stockings of those children with happy, foolish things.

The psalmist says, "The LORD is king! Let the earth rejoice." Why rejoice? In a world of pain and wrongdoing, why do we have "Rejoicing Sunday" in Advent?

We rejoice because God rules the world in wisdom.

My wife, Brenda, and I returned on the old *Queen Mary* from our first visit to the United States. Traveling by oceanliner meant that the amount of luggage we were allowed to carry was unlimited. Among our many suitcases were two bulky parcels from generous friends. They were Christmas gifts, which we knew would thrill our children—remote-controlled robots. When the packages were eventually opened, the children were ecstatic! Squeals of delight echoed through the house as the battery-propelled creatures emitted strange noises and flashed impressive colored lights. They were great fun.

Consider those robots. They were incapable of telling a lie, yet they could not be described as honest. Honesty requires a conscious rejection of falsehood. They were incapable of cowardice, yet it was impossible to call them brave. Courage is a virtue that requires a choice. They were incapable of hatred, but this did not mean that they were friendly or loving. To respond in friendship and love implies a choice.

If I ruled the world I would not allow an armed assailant to shoot down children and teachers outside a school. If I ruled the world I would not allow a young minister to die of malignant disease at the age of forty, leaving a brokenhearted widow, two fatherless children, and unfinished work. I would suspend all natural laws without a second thought and banish illness. If given the chance, surely that is how all people of compassion would act.

With a God who thinks and acts like us, we would have heaven on earth—or would we? If we look closer, the picture is not so attractive. If God were to intervene and stop a plane from falling out of the sky and killing all its occupants, then God would have to prevent every plane from doing so—because God loves us all equally. This would mean that suddenly and without warning the laws of gravity on which the universe is based would be suspended. The results would be catastrophic.

In a world without dependable natural laws there could be no knowledge, no science, no understanding of the universe, no progress. It would be a world of the inexplicable and the unknowable, a world of superstition and magic. Far from being a heaven, such a world would be a nightmare! My world, were I to rule it, would become a dark, terrifying place with no reason and no free will. There would be no love because there would be no possibility of hatred. There could be no virtue, no development of character, and no possibility of the growth of a soul. For all its shadows, its heartbreaks, and its pain, this world is ruled by the God who came in Jesus—and he rules in wisdom.

Like most children, I loved to fly a kite when I was young. After I had saved up enough pocket money, I would go to the corner shop and buy colored tissue paper. I would paste the paper across a frame my father had made. I would then take it into the park, launch it against the April wind, and watch it struggle in the sky as though trying to break free of the cord which held it prisoner as it explored the heavens.

Suppose I decided to give my kite its liberty? What if, in answer to its struggles, I let the cord go and allowed the kite to soar away? When this happened by accident one day, the kite did not fly higher. Instead it lurched from side to side like a drunken thing before plunging to the earth, broken and helpless. The cord which appeared to hold it prisoner was in fact allowing it to climb.

Our world is not a playground; it is a school which, like the kite cord, is designed to give us the capacity to develop until our spirit is able to take wings. My world, were I in charge, would be designed for pleasure and not for spiritual growth, and in the end it would provide neither. On this third Sunday in Advent, "Rejoicing Sunday," the church celebrates the rule of God. It affirms that the universe is in the hands of the God who came as a baby to Bethlehem and who will come again to bring all things to completion. We rejoice because God rules the world in wisdom.

We rejoice because God rules the world in righteousness.

Judgment has slipped out of Christian preaching because of the misunderstandings of a former day. Deep in people's minds, however, remain the popular conceptions of wrath and torment. It was almost as though God, whom we had cheated during life, would extract revenge after our death. Small wonder then that many Christians have dismissed the concept of judgment altogether.

It is very interesting that the attitude in the book of Psalms is entirely different. There we read of devout people actually longing for judgment. It is as though they are pushing against the door of the celestial courtroom, clamoring for admittance so that they might be judged. This coming judgment is a cause for celebration in which even nature shares: "Then shall all the trees of the forest sing for joy / before the LORD; for he is coming, / for he is coming to judge the earth. / He will judge the world with righteousness, / and the peoples with his truth" (Ps. 96:12-13). Judgment in the mind of the psalmist is an occasion for universal rejoicing.

23

The psalmist is thinking not of a vindictive judgment but of one that is tempered with mercy. For the Christian, however, it is even more wonderful than that! The message of Advent is that the God who comes to be our judge loves us, and in Jesus that loving nature is revealed. We have the promise that we will appear before the judgment seat of Christ. This is marvelous news! We will not be judged by society; its judgment can be cruelly superficial. We shall not even judge ourselves, for some of us, driven by a sense of guilt, find it difficult to forgive our own wrongdoing. We will be judged by Christ. This is not a threat but a wonderful promise. Our judge is one who loves us enough to die for us, and there are nail prints in his hands! In Advent we rejoice because God has come in Christ and sees not only our failings but also our hidden struggles to live more noble and unselfish lives. Everything is to be made known; we will not be able to hide anything. And God, who searches the heart, looks upon us with love and understanding.

In one of his addresses to Oxford students, William Temple, a distinguished Archbishop of Canterbury, described the world as being like a shop window where some mischievous person has crept in overnight and changed all the price labels. As a result, cheap things have been given high prices, and the really valuable things are marked down and thrown among the cheap goods. Fame, money, physical beauty, power, and pleasure have all been marked high. Truth, goodness, unselfishness, humility, and purity have all been marked low. And the sad thing is that we have been deceived by it.

Christians believe, however, that when God judges the world in Jesus, all this will be changed. The tags will be reassigned. Those things which are lovely, honorable, just, pure, or gracious (Phil. 4:8) will be given their rightful place. We rejoice, therefore, because God rules the world in righteousness.

We rejoice because God rules the world in love and power.

In my work as a hospital doctor I once admitted a patient suffering from dehydration following prolonged vomiting. It was thought that she had some kind of food poisoning. All the tests, however, proved negative. No cause for the sickness could be found. On her third day in the hospital, I noticed a very slight difference between the reflexes of her right and left legs. This new development opened up a different road of investigation, which led to a sad conclusion.

I groaned as I read the contents of the report from the pathologist which confirmed my fears. The patient was only thirty-four years old. She was sitting up in bed, looking so very much better, when I went to see her. I noticed the photograph of her husband and their three children beside her bed along with her Bible reading notes. We talked about faith, home, and church. I prayed for guidance as I broke the news that she was suffering from multiple sclerosis. Then as never before I experienced what is perhaps the greatest mental anguish in the practice of medicine: to make an accurate diagnosis but not be able to offer a cure.

Thank God the Christian is not in this position. The diagnosis—sin at the heart of the human condition—is accompanied by the knowledge that God has done something about it. There is little point in drawing attention to human defects unless a cure can be offered. Advent is a time of rejoicing because Jesus came not just to draw attention to our sins but, in love and power, to make an end of them forever. It is common to hear people say, "You have to accept me as I am." The glad message of Advent is, "Yes, indeed, you are loved and accepted as you are." But the message does not end there. It goes on to add that in the coming of Jesus we are incorporated into a new creation, and through grace we may begin to be changed into the divine likeness.

One day a teenager was led into my office by my secretary. He wore motorcycling gear and held a crash helmet in his hands. In a hesitant, nervous manner he said, "I think you have someone named Cartwright who belongs to your church, and I wonder if you would let me have his address." I was reluctant to give the address of one of my church members to a stranger, so I asked, "Why do you want it?" The young man shuffled uneasily, and then said, "I sold him a motorbike three months ago. At the time I did not tell him there was a crack in the frame. Now I want to give him his money back." As he said this he took out of his pocket a bundle of banknotes.

My curiosity was aroused. "Why do you want to do that?" I asked. The teenager then explained, "Last week I went to a Billy Graham crusade. I responded to the invitation and came forward to accept Christ. Now I want to put things right."

The church member later told me that he would never forget the sight of that young man standing at his front door with a bundle of banknotes in his hands. He added, "That said more about the power of the gospel than a hundred sermons."

None of us need to stay as we are. There is always the possibility of change, because God is in the life-transforming business. God rules the world in love and power. The Third Sunday in Advent is "Rejoicing Sunday" because God is in control. The *Lord* is king! Let the earth rejoice!

STUDY QUESTIONS

1. Read Isaiah 61. This passage reminds us that our own salvation is not an end in itself but the beginning of a life of service. In what ways can you make this Advent a season of rejoicing for someone else by responding to the various parts of the call in verses 1-3?

2. Read Psalm 126. The returning exiles were overwhelmed by joy as they journeyed back to Jerusalem. What reasons for joy have you found in your Advent journey so far? What would you say are the main differences between "seasonal pleasures" and Advent joy?

3. Advent is a time of rejoicing because we are reminded that we live in a world that is in the hands of God. What would you have said to the young woman in the hospital? Consider the helpful things which might be said to those you know who find it hard to reconcile belief in a good God with the presence of bad things in the world.

4. Read Philippians 4:4-9. How much of your Advent rejoicing is based on your present conditions, and how much rests on an understanding of God and God's ways?

5. Think of those who find it hard to rejoice this Advent—the hurt, the oppressed, the victims of discrimination. What is on your agenda for helping them? Is there any danger of Advent joy becoming a selfish preoccupation? What can you do about it?

FOCUS FOR THE WEEK: ADVENT REJOICING

Advent joy needs to be shared if it is to be experienced to the full. Be mindful of those who find it difficult to believe in the goodness of God because of painful experiences. Consider ways of helping such people in gentle and sensitive ways. Share with them the things which have sustained and encouraged you through your dark days. Devote some time each day to praying for those who find it hard to rejoice and for those who are serving such people in difficult places.

Is God Asleep?

When the fullness of time had come, God sent his Son, born of a woman, born under the law, in order to redeem those who were under the law, so that we might receive adoption as children. (Gal. 4:4-5)

One of my most memorable preaching experiences was unplanned. Some years ago I was invited to be a member of the reception committee for a distinguished elderly scholar who was to preach at a special midweek service scheduled to begin at 12:45 P.M. The appointed hour arrived, but not the preacher; and I was called upon at the last minute to take his place.

As I was leaving the building after the service, I found myself looking into the friendly face of an elderly clergyman who had just arrived. I recognized him from his photograph as our missing preacher. Seeing my clerical collar, he seized my hand and said, "Would you please lead me to the preacher's study?" I stared at him without moving. "Come along," he said in a commanding voice and preceded me up the stairs. I chased after him trying in vain to explain. He was in no mood to listen. "Now come along, young man," he insisted, "or we'll be late for the service."

I took him to the preacher's study. Of course it was deserted. He looked around in bewilderment. "Where is everybody?" he inquired. When I explained, he looked puzzled. "But what time is it? My train arrived just before noon, and the station is only a ten-minute walk from here." "It is two o'clock," I replied. For a moment he looked surprised, and then he realized what had happened. "Why bless my soul!" he exclaimed. "I must be getting old. Do you know what I have done? I had a cup of tea in the station restaurant and I must have dozed off for an hour." We subsequently arranged another date, and I made sure that I was there to meet his train. Some lessons don't have to be learned twice!

A recurrent nightmare of the ancients was that God might fall asleep. Elijah taunted the priests of Baal on the summit of Mount Carmel. "Cry louder," he mocked. "Perhaps your god has fallen asleep." How awful if the one who is supposed to be our shield and protector falls asleep and is indifferent to our needs! The psalmist expresses confidence in the Sovereign Lord with the words, "He who keeps Israel / will neither slumber nor sleep" (Ps. 121:4).

All of us have dark nights of the soul when we cry out to heaven, "Why is this happening? Is God asleep?" I remember holding three-year-old

Sharon in my arms, her heartbroken mother looking on. Sharon was one of my patients and was suffering from a cerebral tumor. She was blind, frightened, and crying in distress. Her mother, knowing my Christian convictions, whispered in anguish, "Can't God do something about this?"

Such a question arises out of a bewildered sense that life is no longer morally intelligible. When good people suffer in spite of love and faithfulness, the foundations of faith seem to quake. "What is going on?" we cry. "Is God asleep?" As we approach Bethlehem, the church celebrates its conviction that in the coming of Jesus, the Kingdom of eternity has broken into time. God's activity in Christ is clear evidence that God is eternally vigilant and not asleep.

We celebrate God's moment.

"When the fullness of time had come . . . " (Gal. 4:4)

As I make my way to my study, I pass a large, framed photograph of my daughter on her wedding day. It brings back one moment in particular. It was the wedding day morning. In marked contrast to the bustling excitement of the preceding weeks, which rose to crescendo in the last few frantic days, the house was still and quiet. Everyone had left for the church. I stood in the hall of our home waiting for my daughter to come down the stairs; then we would set off together for the church in our traditional way.

All the preparations were complete. At that moment all were in their appointed places. The organist was playing the music. The ushers were on duty. The assisting ministers, the bridesmaids, and the bride's mother were all at the church. Control was now out of my hands. All I could do was wait. And then, finally, radiantly, she came down the stairs. It was an unforgettable moment when I realized that the waiting was over. The moment had come.

The faithful people of God knew all about waiting. Through the long years of national humiliation, they believed God's promise of a deliverer, and they waited. When the brutal Assyrians ravaged their land, descending like wolves on the fold, they believed and waited. When Nebuchadnezzar the Babylonian invaded and desecrated God's Temple, the faithful few believed and waited. When the Greeks came with all the blandishments of their culture, devout men and women resisted; they believed and waited. When the Romans came with trumpets and banners, they believed and waited.

The foolish old man drags his aching limbs up the temple steps each morning. For years he has carried out the same daily routine. He is convinced that he will not die until the day of waiting is over and he sees

God's promised Deliverer. He scrutinizes each couple who bring their firstborn son to the temple, stumbling forward so that he might catch a glimpse of each child's face.

Then one day a strong working man and his very young wife come from the North. Old Simeon looks at Mary and with trembling hands moves back the swaddling cloth so that his gaze may linger on the child. In his eyes comes a seraphic faraway look. Suddenly, he knows that the long vigil has ended; the waiting is over. "Lord, now lettest thou thy servant depart in peace . . . for mine eyes have seen thy salvation" (Luke 2:29-30 KJV).

Caesar Augustus and Herod may have thought they were making history, but that old man weeping over a little baby will be remembered when all their talk of empires is stilled. Simeon realizes the curtain is rising on the final act of creation. A new heaven and a new earth are coming into being. The waiting is over.

Paul says, "When the fullness of time had come." In Advent we celebrate God's choice of God's own moment. When Jesus came, the known world was joined by the common Greek language so that Paul and the other preachers would be understood wherever they preached. The straight Roman roads provided ready routes along which the ambassadors of Christ could travel. Pompey had swept the Mediterranean of pirates so that the Christian missionaries could pass freely and safely. The *Pax Romana* held the world together. The right time had come. The waiting was over. The moment was of God's choosing, and it was right.

The message of Advent rings out to all who labor and are heavy laden, and to all who are downcast with grief and heartbreak. God never sleeps but is eternally vigilant, and God has been preparing for the right moment. Advent declares that God has shared humanity's hopes, hurts, and disappointments, and the waiting is now over. The time has fully come. In the birth of Jesus in Bethlehem, God has come to heal, to forgive, and to bless. We celebrate the coming of Jesus as the moment when the Kingdom of heaven broke into time. We celebrate also the continuing presence of Christ in the church through the Holy Spirit, and we look forward in hopeful anticipation to the second Advent when this work will be finally completed.

We celebrate God's method.

"God sent his Son, born of a woman, born under the law . . ." (Gal. 4:4)

My first automobile was a source of pride and joy. Once when I was cleaning the inside, I found a book under the driver's seat with the title *The Owner's Maintenance Manual.* Although the car was already several years old when I bought it, this book was still in immaculate condition. It introduced me to a fascinating new vocabulary—crankshafts, differentials, valve clearances, sump oil, and the like. In the manual I read, "In the event of a loss of power you may find that the points need adjusting." I immediately decided that my car lacked power, and I went in search of the unsuspecting points. The book informed me that these would be found by removing the distributor head. The instruction was to turn a particular screw. I did so and found my hand filled with pieces from the distributor!

In vain I searched for advice on what to do next. After an hour of trial and error, I went to the telephone, hands covered in grease, and dialed the mechanic who normally serviced our car in his spare time. I confessed that I had tried to adjust the points. He did not seem enthusiastic about my excursion into automobile engineering, but he patiently told me what to do. I thought I understood. With his words ringing in my ears, I returned to the car but I discovered that what he had told me was not enough. After fifteen frustrating minutes I returned to the telephone in despair. An exasperated voice said, "Don't do anything else. Just wait there and I will come."

There are moments when what is required is not a lesson but a rescue. Advent is the time when we celebrate God's method in responding to our plight by coming in Jesus. Our Advent celebration is an affirmation that God is not remote. As Mary and Joseph make their way to Bethlehem, Christians declare that in what is about to happen God is shown to be no cosmic clockmaker who wound the world up and then abandoned it to its fate. In the child lying in a manger we celebrate a God who comes and stands alongside us, ever wakeful—who comes to rescue us in Jesus.

God's response to our plight is not more instruction but a personal appearance. During Advent we celebrate the astonishing news that for our sake God took human form as a humbly born baby. Advent is much more than the celebration of a past event; it is also the celebration of a present experience. God's rescue, in love and forgiveness, is repeated whenever a person turns and receives Christ through faith.

We celebrate God's motive.

"In order to redeem those who were under the law, so that we might receive adoption as children." (Gal. 4:5)

A committee on which I once served was considering the future of a young man. He had been foolish. He had drifted into bad company, had brought sorrow and embarrassment to his family, and had compromised his employer. As we considered the right course of action, one of our number, a woman of great compassion, said, "What this young man needs is a clean sheet, and we ought to be big enough to give him one." I was proud of my colleagues. They immediately endorsed this suggestion and gave him a second chance. As a result he made a fresh start and justified our trust by making good. Since then he has given valuable service to many worthy causes. He has been "redeemed."

Our daily experiences remind us that a clean sheet is needed because the old one is badly defaced. We watch familiar tragedies unfolding on our television screens: the wreckage from a car bomb, a bewildered family crying around an open grave, lines of starving people, stories of cruelty and selfishness.

A patient of mine, a dear trusting soul, had a magnificent grandfather clock in her hall. I had to squeeze past it each time I paid a house call. Its mechanism needed overhauling, but that would not have been very expensive. It had a beautifully engraved brass face. I could see that it was an antique, and I assumed my patient was aware of its value. One day I called and it was gone. "Where's the clock?" I asked. She replied with a smile, "Oh, two nice young men came and exchanged it for that lovely clock there on the mantelpiece." I looked at the cheap timepiece they had left and felt anger rising up inside. To think that men could be so mean as to rob a poor trusting woman!

I know of a young woman dying of AIDS. She did not know her husband was being unfaithful. She made that terrible discovery when she found that he had passed on to her the infection. She is trying so hard not to be bitter. Understandably she is not finding it easy. She feels that she is being robbed of most of her life, and it breaks her heart to think of her children growing up without their mother.

Wouldn't it be wonderful to have a clean sheet and start afresh with good men and women? That is why in Advent we celebrate God's motive for coming in Jesus, which was to bring to birth a new kind of person, described by Paul as "a new creation" (2 Cor. 5:17). Through the Holy Spirit, God gives us a clean sheet. The work of re-creation continues, and one day this will be completed when Jesus returns to bring in the full glory of the Kingdom.

Celebrate Advent; don't miss out on the miracle!

STUDY QUESTIONS

1. Read Isaiah 11:1-9. The Messiah whom the prophet foresees will not only bring justice for humankind but will also transform the natural order. How can we cooperate with God in the re-creation of our environment? Should the wise and just use of the earth's resources be considered part of our Christian stewardship? If so, what specific things can we do about it?

2. Read Luke 1:47-55. Try not to allow your familiarity with these words of Mary's song to obscure their dramatic message. Mary recognizes that she is of low estate, yet God uses her. What other instances in both biblical and more recent times has God used "nobodies" to accomplish the purposes of the Kingdom? Do we give adequate recognition to the role Mary played in the gospel story? What does this story have to say to you about your surrender to the will of God?

3. Read Revelation 21:1-7. How much of our Christian experience and hope is already fulfilled and how much lies in the future? What practical things can you do this Christmas to make the promises of this passage true for others?

4. Have you ever been tempted to think that God is indifferent to your personal needs, that God is asleep? What have you found most helpful in reassuring yourself of God's continual presence and love in your life? How can you use your own experience to help others who are going through a similar eclipse of faith?

FOCUS FOR THE WEEK: ADVENT, A TIME OF CELEBRATION

Christmas is near and festivities are about to begin. Bring all your Advent preparation into your celebration so that it will be not only a social but also a *spiritual* experience. To be mindful of the spiritual dimension will enhance, not diminish, the joy and gladness of the season. Let the wonder of God's amazing love shown in the coming of Jesus cast its radiance over all your seasonal activities. Remember that this is a time of celebration because of what God has done.